This Orchard book
belongs to

_____

_____

_____

For Joe and James,
the original Littlebob and Plum! G.P-R.

ORCHARD BOOKS
338 Euston Road, London, NW1 3BH
Orchard Books Australia
17/207 Kent Street, Sydney, NSW 2000

First published in 2010 by Orchard Books
First published in paperback in 2011

Text and illustrations © Guy Parker-Rees 2010

ISBN: 978 1 40830 420 4

A CIP catalogue record for this book
is available from the British Library.

Printed in China

2 4 6 8 10 9 7 5 3 1

Orchard Books is a division of Hachette Children's Books,
an Hachette UK company.

www.hachette.co.uk

Playtime
with
Littlebob and Plum

Guy Parker-Rees

ORCHARD BOOKS

Look! Littlebob and Plum are playing hide-and-seek.

Quick! Hide, Plum!

6 7 8 9 . . .

10! **Coming to find you!**

Where can she be, Littlebob?

Try again, Plum.
Find the perfect
hiding place.

Hurry up! Littlebob is coming!

Try over there, Plum!

Plum has hidden just in time!
Can you find her, Littlebob?

It's your turn to seek, Plum.
Can you count up to ten?

1 2 3 4 5 6

Off you go –
find Littlebob!

It's your turn to seek, Plum.
Can you count up to ten?

1 2 3 4 5 6

Off you go –
find Littlebob!

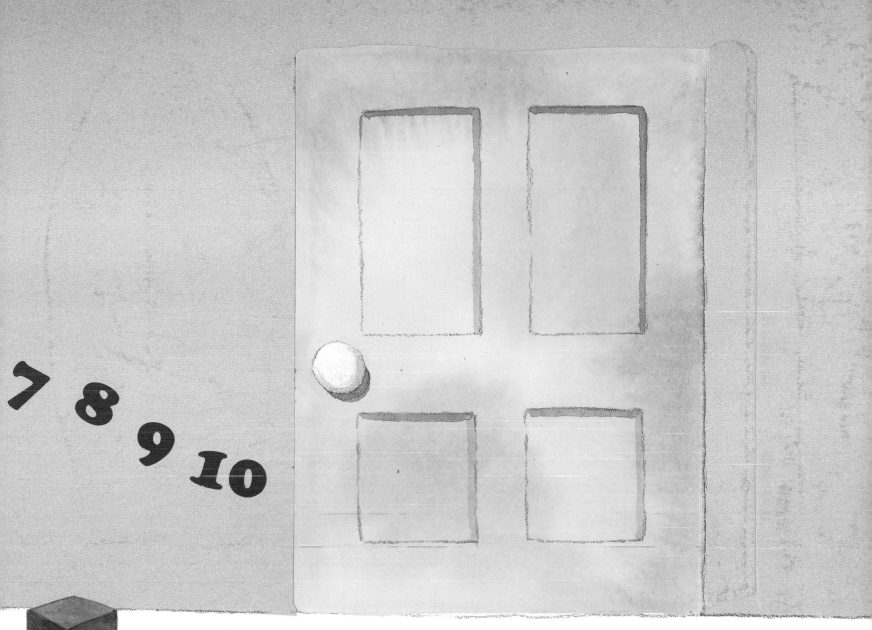

7 8 9 10

Oh, not too fast . . .

Ouch!

**Poor Plum.
Did you
fall over?**

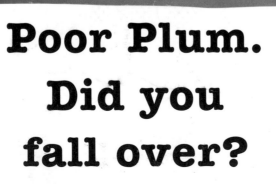

Littlebob will give you a hug better. Can you find him?

Keep looking . . .

There's one last
place to try . . .

**Big hug!
All better
now, Plum.**

Perhaps that's enough hide-and-seek for today.

Do you think the rain has stopped? Let's see . . .